:thelwell.
GOES WEST

thelwell.
GOES WEST

EYRE METHUEN

First published in 1975
by Eyre Methuen Ltd
11 New Fetter Lane, London EC4P 4EE
Copyright © 1975 by Norman Thelwell

ISBN 0 413 34400 2

Printed in Great Britain
by Whitstable Litho, Straker Brothers Ltd

CONTENTS

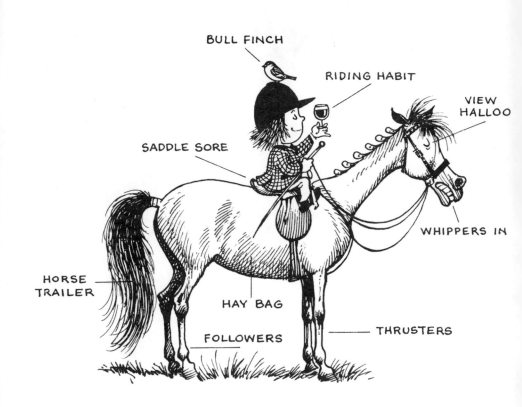

BULL FINCH

RIDING HABIT

VIEW HALLOO

SADDLE SORE

WHIPPERS IN

HORSE TRAILER

HAY BAG

THRUSTERS

FOLLOWERS

THE ENGLISH RIDER

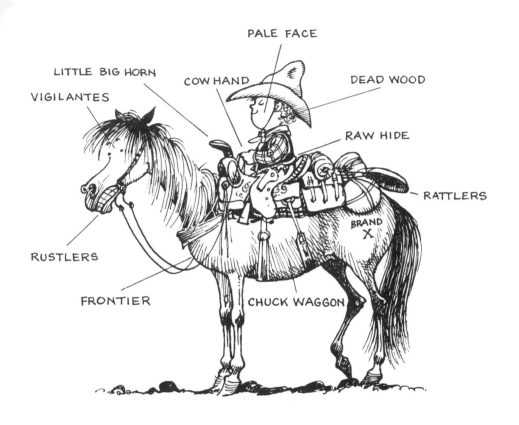

PALE FACE

LITTLE BIG HORN

COW HAND

DEAD WOOD

VIGILANTES

RAW HIDE

RATTLERS

BRAND X

RUSTLERS

FRONTIER

CHUCK WAGGON

THE WESTERN HORSEMAN

WESTERN RIDING

BEFORE TAKING UP WESTERN RIDING – IT IS IMPORTANT TO STUDY THE COWBOY SEAT

IN THE WEST, RIDERS FIND IT MORE COMFORTABLE TO SIT AS LOW AS POSSIBLE IN THE SADOLE —

AND TO KEEP ONE HAND FREE OF THE REINS AT ALL TIMES

ASK THEM TO SHOW YOU THEIR HANDS, WHEN YOU GET A CHANCE AND –

NOTICE THE RELAXED POSITION ADOPTED BY MOST COWBOYS WHEN RIDING THE RANGE

— OR WHEN THEY HIT TOWN

13

THE EASTERN RIDER LIKES TO BUMP UP AND DOWN IN THE SADDLE

THIS IS ALL VERY WELL OVER SHORT DISTANCES

BUT REMEMBER —

THE COW-HAND MAY BE ON THE TRAIL FOR WEEKS AT A TIME

WHEN COMMUNICATING HIS WISHES TO HIS HORSE, THE COWBOY
DOES SO VIA THE ANIMAL'S NECK

SOME ENGLISH METHODS ARE NOT CONSIDERED GOOD PRACTICE

WHEN OUT ON THE RANGE —

YOUR SURVIVAL MAY WELL DEPEND UPON YOUR PONY'S NATURAL COURAGE —

AND SUREFOOTEDNESS

SO TREAT HIM LIKE A FRIEND

WHAT TO WEAR

THE RIDERS OF THE WEST ARE EASY-GOING, OUTDOOR
GUYS AND GALS AND LOVE TO TRAVEL LIGHT —

THEY PRIDE THEMSELVES ON THEIR SIMPLE AND PRACTICAL FORM OF DRESS

AND ARE INCLINED TO GREET FANCY CLOTHES WITH AMUSEMENT

THE SADDLE IS HEAVIER AND MORE COMPLICATED THAN YOU MAY HAVE BEEN USED TO —

SO MAKE SURE YOU KNOW HOW TO PUT IT ON CORRECTLY

WHEN DONE BY AN EXPERT, IT ALL LOOKS VERY SIMPLE

DON'T FORGET TO TIGHTEN UP THE CINCHES

WESTERN HORSES

THE MUSTANG

KNOWN THE WORLD OVER FOR HIS UNIQUE CONTRIBUTION TO
THE MOTION PICTURE INDUSTRY, THIS LOVABLE HORSE HAS
APPEARED IN MORE FILMS THAN BILLY-THE-KID

THE QUARTER HORSE

HAS GREAT CATTLE SENSE AND IS ABLE TO GET OFF THE
MARK WITH ASTONISHING SPEED

THE BRONCO

HIS NAME COMES FROM THE SPANISH WORD MEANING ROUGH & RUDE

THE PINTO
OR PAINTED HORSE

NATURAL CAMOUFLAGE GAVE THIS ANIMAL A GREAT ADVANTAGE IN BATTLE
HE WAS MUCH FAVOURED BY THE INDIANS WHEN ON THE WAR-PATH —

SO WAS THE **APALOOSA** OR SPOTTED HORSE

THE AMERICAN SADDLE HORSE

FAMOUS FOR HIS ABILITY TO EXECUTE AN ASTONISHING VARIETY
OF SPECTACULAR GAITS

THE MORGAN HORSE

THIS STRIKING LITTLE ANIMAL HAS LEFT HIS IMPRINT
ON ALMOST EVERY OTHER AMERICAN BREED

THE PALOMINO

KNOWN AS THE GOLDEN HORSE OF THE WEST, THIS HANDSOME CREATURE
IS POPULAR WITH ALL THOSE WHO APPRECIATE NATURAL BEAUTY

QUICK ON THE DRAWL

TO UNDERSTAND THE COWBOY'S WAY OF LIFE IT IS ADVISABLE TO KNOW THE MEANING OF CERTAIN WORDS AND PHRASES MUCH USED BY THE EXPERTS

HERE ARE A FEW :-

TENDER FOOT (OR HOP-A-LONG)

SIDE KICKS

THE LONE STRANGER

A SOD BUSTER OR —

GETTING YOURSELF A LITTLE SPREAD

SPEAKING WITH FORKED TONGUE

HIGH NOON

GETTING THE DROP ON A GUY

LOOKING DOWN THE BARREL OF A COLT

GET A LONG LITTLE DOGIE

HOW TO UNDERSTAND YOUR HORSE

HORSES CANNOT TALK . IT IS USEFUL ,THEREFORE, TO HAVE
SOME IDEA OF WHAT THEY MAY BE THINKING

IMPORTANT CLUES TO YOUR PONY'S THOUGHTS MAY BE GLEANED
BY CLOSE OBSERVATION OF HIS EARS

FOR EXAMPLE :—

" I INTEND TO SHOOT OFF TO THE LEFT "

" YOU HAVE SHOT OFF TO THE RIGHT "

" THERE'S A NASTY WIND BLOWING UP "

" MAKE FOR COVER – IT'S A TWISTER "

"I AM GOING TO GALLOP UNDER THIS LOW TREE BRANCH"

" WHAT A DREADFUL NAME TO CALL A PONY "

THE EXPERT CAN READ HIS HORSE FROM BOTH ENDS OF COURSE

" YOU WANT TO CHASE COWS – YOU CHASE COWS "

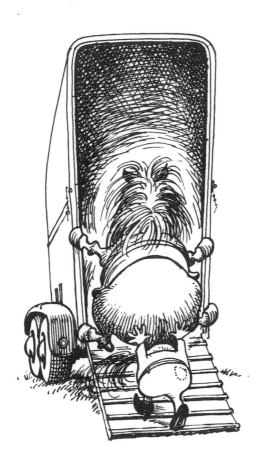

" YOU'LL NEVER GET ME UP IN ONE OF THOSE THINGS"

NOTICE HIS GENERAL DEMEANOUR

YOU WILL SOON LEARN WHAT HE IS TRYING TO SAY :-

" OOH ! OOH ! I'VE TRODDEN ON YOUR GUITAR "

" IT SOUNDED LIKE A RATTLE-SNAKE TO ME "

" IT'S FREEZING OUT THERE ON THE PRAIRIE "

" ALL THIS RIDING OFF INTO THE SUNSET IS RUINING MY EYES"

ON THE TRAIL

BEFORE SADDLING UP - MAKE SURE YOUR HORSE IS
HEALTHY, ALERT AND READY TO GO —

HE SHOULD BE TRAINED TO STEP OVER FALLEN TIMBER WITHOUT HESITATION

AND BE PREPARED TO CARRY EXTRA LOADS WHEN CALLED UPON TO DO SO

HE MUST NOT SPOOK
AT HARMLESS OBJECTS

OR BLUNDER HEADLONG INTO DANGEROUS ONES

DO NOT GET ANXIOUS ON DIFFICULT TERRAIN
— YOU MAY COMMUNICATE YOUR FEELINGS TO YOUR HORSE

AND <u>DON'T</u> LEAN OVER IN THE SADDLE WHEN TIRED

YOU MAY UPSET HIS BALANCE

ALWAYS DISMOUNT ON THE UPHILL
SIDE OF YOUR PONY

AND IF YOU START AN AVALANCHE - SHOUT A WARNING TO RIDERS BELOW

BE PREPARED TO TRUST HIS NATURAL INSTINCTS AND ABILITIES WHEN CROSSING NARROW BRIDGES

AND DO NOT ALLOW HIM INTO WATER IF HE IS HOT

IN VERY HOT CONDITIONS - ALLOW HIM TO TAKE ADVANTAGE OF ANY
AVAILABLE SHADE

AND RAISE HIS SADDLE FROM TIME TO TIME TO LET THE AIR CIRCULATE

IT IS BAD MANNERS TO RIDE TOO CLOSE TO THE HORSE IN FRONT

OR TO ATTEMPT TO OVERTAKE ON A NARROW TRAIL

AND MOST IMPORTANT OF ALL —

NEVER RIDE OVER PRIVATE PROPERTY WITHOUT FIRST OBTAINING
THE OWNER'S CONSENT

How to Manage a Mean Horse

REFUSING TO BE CAUGHT

THIS CAN BE VERY TRYING. DECOY HIM TO SOME CONVENIENT SPOT AND BE READY TO SLIP A ROPE OVER HIS HEAD WITHOUT AROUSING HIS SUSPICION

MOVING OFF WHEN ABOUT TO BE MOUNTED

AN EXASPERATING HABIT. TRY THE OLD INDIAN TRICK OF LEADING HIM INTO A BOG AND MOUNTING UP WHILST HIS MOVEMENT IS RESTRICTED

BLANKET TEARING

HE IS PROBABLY BORED — TRY SINGING A DIFFERENT SONG

VIOLENT PULLING ON THE REINS

THIS CAN UNSEAT A RIDER -

HAVE A LOOK AT HIS MOUTH - HE MAY HAVE SORE TEETH

CRIB BITING

THE ANIMAL SHOULD BE ISOLATED - THE HABIT IS CATCHING

WIND SUCKING

GET RID OF THE HORSE – THE RESULTS CAN BE ALARMING

BITING

CAN OFTEN BE CURED - STOP CARRYING SUGAR LUMPS IN YOUR
BACK POCKET

SUDDEN REARING

THE ANSWER HERE IS TO SLIP OUT OF THE SADDLE WHENEVER HE DOES IT

ROLLING

THIS IS NATURAL TO A HORSE AND ONE OF HIS CHIEF JOYS

DO NOT LET IT DEPRESS YOU

BOLTING

TRY JERKING HIS HEAD VIOLENTLY BACKWARDS AND FORWARDS
BY PULLING ON THE REINS - THE IDEA HERE IS THAT IT
WILL TEND TO CONFUSE HIM

KICKING

MAY WELL BE CAUSED BY NERVOUSNESS - TRY TO COMFORT AND REASSURE HIM

SAVAGING

A FRIGHTENING SIGHT - DROP EVERYTHING - RUN LIKE A JACK RABBIT

HOW TO CROSS WATER

DO NOT TRY TO FORCE HIM INTO THE WATER AGAINST HIS WILL

DEMONSTRATE TO HIM THAT THE WATER IS HARMLESS

HE WILL GO IN WHEN HE IS READY

DO NOT DISMOUNT AND LEAD HIM FROM IN FRONT

HE IS LIKELY TO CLIMB ON TO ANYTHING THAT LOOKS SOLID

MAKE SURE YOU KNOW HOW TO
ADMINISTER THE KISS OF LIFE —

YOU NEVER KNOW WHO MAY NEED IT

RODEO DOUGH

A GREAT DEAL OF MONEY GOES INTO THE RODEO RING THESE DAYS
SO IT IS AS WELL TO STUDY SOME OF THE RULES

PARTICIPANTS ARE EXPECTED TO BE REASONABLY COMPETENT BEFORE ENTERING
THE ARENA

AND TO PERFORM A PATTERN OF MOVEMENT EXACTLY AS
SPECIFIED BY THE JUDGES

SOME RIDERS CHOOSE TO
DEMONSTRATE THEIR SKILL
IN THE SADDLE

SOME PERFORM BAREBACK

OTHERS APPEAR TO BE HAPPIER ON A BULL

EACH RIDER MUST STAY
ABOARD FOR A SPECIFIED
NUMBER OF SECONDS

AND MUST RAKE THE SHOULDERS
OF HIS MOUNT CONTINUOUSLY
WITH HIS HEELS

ON NO ACCOUNT MUST HE TOUCH HIS HORSE WITH HIS HANDS

A MILD MANNERED ANIMAL MAY COST HIM VALUABLE POINTS —

BUT EXTRA MARKS MAY BE AWARDED FOR STYLE

IN CASE OF DOUBT —

THE COMPETITOR MAY BE ASKED TO REPEAT HIS PERFORMANCE

WESTERN QUIZ

Q. WHY IS THIS COWBOY SHOOTING UP THE TOWN ?

A. BECAUSE HIS HORSE STOPPED SUDDENLY ON MAIN STREET

Q.   IS THIS GUY A BRONCO BUSTER?

A. NO, BUT HE SOON WILL BE IF HE GOES ON FEEDING CORN AT THAT RATE

Q. STUDY THIS PICTURE. HOW CAN YOU TELL THAT THIS IS A BAD MAN ?

A. HE HAS NEGLECTED TO CHECK HIS HORSE'S FEET FOR ROCKS

Q. WHAT IS MEANT BY THE EXPRESSION 'WINDY DRAWS'?

A. IT IS A TERM OF CONTEMPT FOR NERVOUS COWBOYS

Q.   THIS PONY HAS FOUR WEAK POINTS - WHAT ARE THEY ?

A.   HIS LEGS

A. THE HEAD SHOULD BE UP AND THE HEELS DOWN

Q. IS THIS COWPOKE BEING CHASED BY A POSSE?

A. NO. THE CORRECT NAME IS COUGAR OR MOUNTAIN LION

Q. WHY IS THIS RIDER LOOKING UNCOMFORTABLE ?

A. HIS JEANS ARE TOO TIGHT

Q. WOULD YOU CALL THIS GUY A SADDLE TRAMP?

A. IF IT WAS YOUR SADDLE YOU WOULD

Q   WHAT IS WRONG WITH THIS PICTURE?

A.   THE RIDER HAS GOT THE WRONG FOOT IN THE STIRRUP

Q. WHAT IMPORTANT RULE DID THIS RIDER NEGLECT ?

A. SHE DID NOT CHECK THE BRAND BEFORE BUYING HER PONY.

AND FINALLY — WHAT IS THE MOST IMPORTANT RULE TO REMEMBER?

THAT'S RIGHT! <u>NEVER</u> HOLD ONTO THE REINS WITH BOTH HANDS